PUPIL TASK CARDS

There are 10 Pupil Task Cards

1. Opportunity Knocks!
2. Getting Personal
3. Getting Going and Getting Over It
4. Getting Down to Specifics
5. The Highs and Lows of Exercise
6. Healthy Heart Happenings
7. Major Muscle Movements
8. Muscling in on Your Health
9. Performing a Balancing Act
10. Maximising the Benefits - Minimising the Risks

Each card is double-sided, appropriately illustrated and includes:

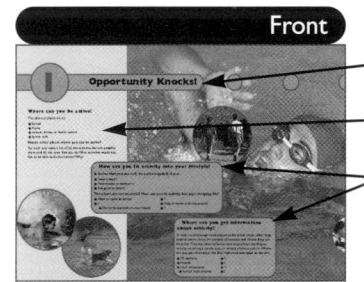

Front
- The card number and title
- Information about a topic
- Questions for pupils to consider and answer during the lesson

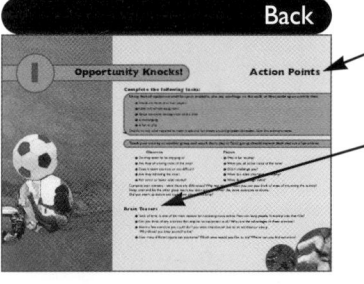

Back
- **Action Points**: Tasks involving physical activity *(approximately 30 minutes duration)* to be performed during the lesson
- **Brain Teasers**: Questions on the topic which can be addressed in the lesson by all pupils *(whole class or small group activity)*, or given as extension tasks for some pupils, or as homework for the whole class

Content

The 10 cards cover the following main topics:

Activity Promotion (Cards 1 and 2)
Preparation and Recovery (Cards 3 and 4)
Cardiovascular Health (Cards 5 and 6)
Musculo-Skeletal Health (Cards 7 and 8)
Energy Balance (Card 9)
Safety (Card 10)

Using the Cards

Cards can be used flexibly within: HRE units of work, areas of activity, PSE lessons, all of these.

See pages 5-6 for more guidance on this.
Within any of the above settings, the cards can be made use of in a number of different ways
- **the teacher uses the card(s)** to help plan units and lessons and, if desired, to design a pupil booklet or pupil worksheets (these can be completed during and/or after lessons)
- **pupils use the card(s)** in lessons as a 'hands-on' resource eg one card is photocopied and used by all pupils in a class or different cards on the same or a similar topic are used by different groups within a class.

LEARNING OUTCOMES

The specific **Learning Outcomes** for each of the ten cards are detailed below.

Card	Learning Outcomes
	Pupils should:
1 Opportunity Knocks!	Know the full range of activity opportunities and ways of incorporating exercise into everyday life; be able to access information about a wide range of activity opportunities.
2 Getting Personal	Be active for 60 minutes per day *(in and out of school)*; be aware of and able to monitor and evaluate personal activity levels over a period of time.
3 Getting Going and Getting Over It	Know and understand the value of preparing for and recovering from activity and the purpose of each of the components of a warm-up and a cool-down; be able to plan and perform parts of a warm-up and a cool-down.
4 Getting Down to Specifics	Be able to plan and perform a safe relevant warm-up and cool-down both for general activity and for a specific activity.
5 The Highs and Lows of Exercise	Be able to plan and perform safe, effective and developmentally-appropriate cardiovascular exercises of varying intensities and impact.
6 Healthy Heart Happenings	Understand and be able to monitor a range of effects of cardiovascular exercise; understand the range of effects of cardiovascular exercise on physical, mental and social health.
7 Major Muscle Movements	Be able to plan and perform safe, effective and developmentally-appropriate musculo-skeletal exercises for the major muscle groups.
8 Muscling in on Your Health	Understand and be able to monitor a range of effects of musculo-skeletal exercise; understand the range of long-term effects of musculo-skeletal exercise on physical, mental and social health.
9 Performing a Balancing Act	Know and understand that whole body activities help to reduce body fat, and that conditioning exercises help to tone muscles; know and understand that increasing activity levels and eating a balanced diet can help to maintain a healthy body weight; know and understand that the body needs a minimum daily energy intake in order to function properly, and that strict dieting and excessive exercising can damage one's health; be able to perform safe, effective and developmentally-appropriate cardiovascular and musculo-skeletal exercises appropriate for maintaining a healthy body weight.
10 Maximising the Benefits - Minimising the Risks	Know how to maximise the health benefits of physical activity; be aware of any risks involved and know how to minimise them.

INTRODUCTION
PUPIL TASK CARDS
TEACHER'S HANDBOOK

This resource is designed to support the delivery of Health Related Exercise (HRE) at Key Stage 3. The content is consistent with the HRE requirements outlined in the 2000 edition of Physical Education in the National Curriculum in Wales and takes account of related requirements from the Personal and Social Education (PSE) curriculum, and relevant aspects of the Science curriculum.

The resource comprises

PUPIL TASK CARDS & TEACHER'S HANDBOOK

The **PUPIL TASK CARDS** are designed to be used by pupils either individually or collectively in groups within lessons. They are task-related and can be used with or without teacher intervention. They can all be used in PE lessons as they each involve practical activity. Within the PE curriculum, they can be utilised within specific units of work on Health Related Exercise, or integrated within appropriate areas of activity. Some of the cards can be used within a PSE programme.

The **TEACHER'S HANDBOOK** is designed to assist teachers in planning and delivering the HRE requirements of the PE curriculum at Key Stage 3. It accompanies the Pupil Task Cards, providing supplementary information to support pupil learning *(including ideas for practical work and answers to the questions on the cards)*, and examples of how the cards can be incorporated within scheme and units of work at Key Stage 3.

Curriculum Requirements

The HRE requirements for Key Stage 3 within Physical Education in The Wales Curriculum 2000 are presented below.

Health Related Exercise

Throughout Key Stage 3, pupils should be taught:

- To monitor a range of short-term effects on the cardiovascular system (*eg changes in heart rate*) and the musculo-skeletal system (*eg changes in muscular strength/endurance and flexibility, improved muscle tone*).

- The long-term effects of exercise on physical health (*eg reduced risk of heart disease, osteoporosis, obesity, improved management of health conditions such as asthma*).

- To adopt good posture when sitting, standing and taking part in activity.

- Relevant and safe warm-up and cool-down routines (*eg mobility exercises, whole-body activities and static stretches*) and how to take responsibility for their planning and execution.

- The differences between whole-body activities that help to reduce body fat and conditioning exercises that improve muscle tone.

- That appropriate training can improve fitness and performance.

- The value of exercise to social and psychological well-being (*eg increased confidence and self-esteem, decreased anxiety and stress*).

- The range of activity opportunities at school, home and in the local community, and ways of incorporating exercise into their lifestyles (*eg walking or cycling to school or to meet friends*).

Pupils should adopt safe practices and procedures when taking part in physical activities that might require the wearing of protective clothing, the removal of jewellery to avoid injury, the supervised use of equipment or response to specific weather conditions.

HEALTHY HEART HAPPENINGS

Health Related Exercise

THE HIGHS AND LOWS OF EXERCISE

GETTING DOWN TO SPECIFICS

MUSCLING IN ON YOUR HEALTH

MAJOR MUSCLE MOVEMENTS

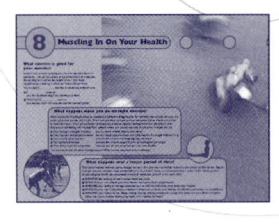

OPPORTUNITY KNOCKS!

GETTING GOING AND GETTING OVER IT

PERFORMING A BALANCING ACT

DR JO HARRIS

TEACHER'S HANDBOOK

LEVEL DESCRIPTION

COMMON REQUIREMENTS AND SKILLS
PUPIL RESPONSES
ASSESSMENT
DIFFERENTIATION

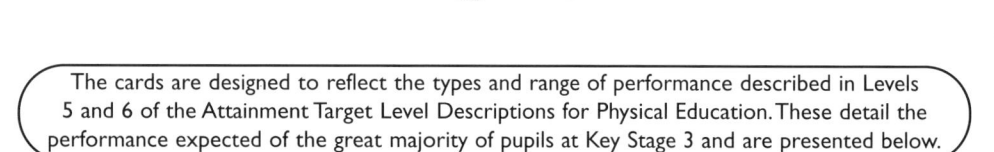

> The cards are designed to reflect the types and range of performance described in Levels 5 and 6 of the Attainment Target Level Descriptions for Physical Education. These detail the performance expected of the great majority of pupils at Key Stage 3 and are presented below.

Level 5
Pupils perform relevant and safe warm-up and cool-down routines and begin to take some responsibility for their planning. They know how to monitor a range of short-term effects on the cardiovascular system and show some understanding of the value of exercise to social and psychological well-being.

Level 6
Pupils recognise the importance of rules and safety procedures and apply them consistently. They take increasing responsibility for the planning and execution of safe exercises, know which exercises to avoid to prevent possible injury, and understand that appropriate training can improve fitness and performance. They understand many of the long-term effects of exercise on physical, mental and social health.

Common Requirements and Skills
Within the cards, issues of access and equity have been considered and opportunities have been taken to develop pupils':
- **Communication Skills** (all cards)
- **Mathematical Skills** (eg Cards 2 and 6)
- **Information Technology Skills** (eg Card 1)
- **Problem-Solving Skills** (all cards)
- **Creative Skills** (eg Cards 1 and 2)
- **Personal and Social Education** (all cards)

Pupil Responses
Pupils will not be able to write responses to questions and tasks on the **Pupil Task Cards**. Any pupil responses will need to be recorded separately (*eg on a piece of paper or worksheet*). Expectations of suitable responses from pupils to questions and tasks are detailed for each **Pupil Task Card** (*see pages 10–30*).

Assessment
Assessment is integral to the resource in that pupils' knowledge, understanding and skills can be assessed by means of their answers to the questions posed throughout the **Pupil Task Cards** and their ability to manage and complete the related practical tasks.

Differentiation
The vast majority, if not all pupils at Key Stage 3 should be able to cope with the questions and tasks on the **Pupil Task Cards**. Most are designed to permit a range of possible answers and solutions. In addition, elements of choice are permitted within many of the Action Points in order to cater for pupils of differing abilities and preferences (*eg Cards 7 and 8 offer a choice of different versions of exercises*).

The Brain Teasers on each card offer additional opportunities for differentiation. Pupils who complete tasks quickly or more easily than others can be moved onto the additional questions in the Brain Teaser section.

KEY STAGE 3 HRE

PROGRESSING LEARNING
SCHEME OF WORK

Schemes and Units of Work

Progressing Learning

The **Pupil Task Cards** are developmental with each one building on previous learning. For example, throughout the 10 cards, pupils gradually take more responsibility for their own warm-ups and cool-downs. The cards are, therefore, designed to be used, where possible, in numerical order (1 to 10). However, the content covers 6 main topics and each of these can be delivered independently.

There are many ways in which the cards can be used to progress pupil learning across the years of the key stage. One possible suggestion is proposed below:

Year 7
- **Preparation and Recovery** (Cards 3 and 4)
- **Cardiovascular Health** (Cards 5 and 6)

Year 8
- **Musculo-Skeletal Health** (Cards 7 and 8)
- **Energy Balance** (Card 9)

Year 9
- **Safety** (Card 10)
- **Activity Promotion** (Cards 1 and 2)

> Nevertheless, it is also possible to cover all of these topics within one year or two years of the key stage.

Scheme of Work

A Key Stage 3 Scheme of Work should provide an outline of the content of the Health Related Exercise component of the Physical Education curriculum and describe how this is to be delivered within the programme for years 7 to 9. An example follows.

During Key Stage 3, pupils learn how to safely and sensibly prepare for and recover from exercise. They also learn about the short-term and long-term effects of exercise (*cardiovascular and musculo-skeletal*) and the role of exercise in establishing and maintaining health (*physical, mental and social*), including a healthy body weight. In addition, they learn how to maximise the benefits of physical activity and minimise the risks, and where and how to make and take opportunities to be active. Finally, they become aware of their own activity levels and how this compares with the recommendations for their age.

The Key Stage 3 requirements are achieved by integrating some of the above concepts through the areas of activity, delivering others through HRE units, and including some within the school's PSE programme (*see below for details*). Every effort is made to ensure close links between the different parts of the programme.

Area of Activity
- **Preparation and Recovery** (Cards 3 and 4)
- **Safety** (Card 10)

HRE Units
- **Cardiovascular Health** (Cards 5 and 6)
- **Musculo-Skeletal Health** (Cards 7 and 8)

PSE
- **Energy Balance** (Card 9)
- **Activity Promotion** (Cards 1 and 2)

TEACHER'S HANDBOOK — Health Related Exercise

UNITS OF WORK

AREAS OF ACTIVITY
HRE UNITS
PSE

> An example '**Area of Activity**' unit of work (*in which HRE is integrated*) and examples of HRE units of work are presented on pages 8 and 9.

HRE Units

Some or all aspects of the HRE component of the PE curriculum can be delivered through specific HRE units. An example of the way in which 'heart health' can be delivered through an HRE unit is presented on page 8. **Pupil Task Cards** 5 and 6 (*on cardiovascular health*) and **Pupil Task Cards** 7 and 8 (*on musculo-skeletal health*) are considered to be particularly suited to delivery through HRE units. However, it is also possible to integrate these topics and concepts through appropriate areas of activity or to incorporate them within the school's PSE programme.

Integrating HRE within Areas of Activity

It is possible to teach aspects of the HRE component of the PE curriculum through some or all of the areas of activity. An example of ways in which the topics 'preparation and recovery' and 'promoting physical activity' can be integrated within a unit of work on invasion games is presented on page 9. **Pupil Task Cards** 3 and 4 (*preparation and recovery*) and **Pupil Task Card** 10 (*maximising the benefits of physical activity and minimising the risks*) are considered to be particularly suitable for use within the areas of activity. However, it is also possible to teach these topics and concepts within specific HRE units or incorporate them within the school's PSE programme.

Incorporating HRE with a PSE Programme

It may be possible to deliver some aspects of the HRE component of the PE curriculum through a school's PSE programme. **Pupil Task Card** 9 (*energy balance*) and **Pupil Task Cards** 1 and 2 (*activity promotion*) are considered to be suitable for delivery through a PSE programme. However, it is also possible to integrate these topics and concepts through appropriate areas of activity or to deliver them within specific HRE units.

Effective Delivery

Whichever way HRE is organised within the curriculum, it is important that:
- **ALL** pupils are taught **ALL** aspects of the HRE programme of study.
- The delivery is **EFFECTIVE**.
- The programme is **COHERENT** and **CO-ORDINATED**.
- The content is **RELEVANT** to the everyday lives of pupils.

The organisation and delivery of HRE should ensure that:
- HRE aspects delivered within areas of activity are **EXPLICIT** and **VISIBLE**.
- The content of HRE units is **LINKED** to that within the areas of activity.
- Any HRE elements incorporated within a PSE programme **CONTAIN LINKS** with the PE curriculum and extra-curricular programme.
- The varying **SHAPES**, **SIZES**, **ABILITIES**, **BACKGROUNDS** and **LIFESTYLES** of pupils are considered and **ADEQUATELY ADDRESSED**.

Example Units of Work

The next two pages provide examples of units of work in which HRE is either delivered within a focused unit of work or integrated within an area of activity.

Health Related Exercise — TEACHER'S HANDBOOK

EXAMPLE HRE UNIT OF WORK

Key Stage 3

Unit: HEART HEALTH
Year 7 or 8 — Duration: 6-8 Hours

Objectives — To enable pupils to:

- Perform a range of safe and effective cardiovascular activities.
- Know and understand the range of short-term effects of exercise on the cardiovascular system.
- Know and understand the range of long-term effects of exercise on the cardiovascular system.
- Know how much cardiovascular activity is recommended for young people.
- Know where they can participate in a range of cardiovascular activities within the community.

National Curriculum Links
Pupils should be taught:

HRE: to monitor a range of short-term effects on the cardiovascular system; the long-term effects of exercise on physical health; relevant and safe warm-up and cool-down routines, and how to take responsibility for their planning and execution; the value of exercise to social and psychological well-being; the range of activity opportunities at school, home and in the local community, and ways of incorporating exercise into their lifestyles.

Learning Outcomes (Pupils should be able to:)	Learning Activities (Opportunities for pupils to:)	Assessment	Resources
1. Perform a range of cardiovascular activities with good technique.	Perform a range of cardiovascular activities (*eg brisk walking, jogging, running, skipping, active games playing, swimming, exercise to music*).	1	As appropriate for the activities (*eg skipping ropes*) PUPIL TASK CARD 5
2. Monitor the short-term effects of cardiovascular exercise.	Perform cardiovascular activities with good technique and understand the consequences of poor technique (*eg jogging and skipping on toes; performing uncontrolled, flinging movements*).	1	As appropriate for the activities, posters PUPIL TASK CARD 5
3. Understand the long-term effects of cardiovascular exercise.	Monitor and explain the range of short-term effects of cardiovascular exercise on physical and mental health (*eg changes in breathing and heart rate, recovery rate, temperature, appearance, skin, feelings, emotions*).	2	Worksheets, posters, monitoring equipment (*eg watch, benches, heart rate monitor, tapes*) PUPIL TASK CARD 6
4. Compare their own activity levels with that recommended for young people.	Explain the range of long-term effects of cardiovascular exercise on physical health (*reduced risk of heart disease, obesity*) and mental health (*increased self-esteem, confidence, companionship*).	3	Posters, worksheets PUPIL TASK CARD 6
5. Know where in the community they can participate in cardiovascular activities.	Develop their awareness of how much cardiovascular activity is recommended for young people (*60 minutes of at least moderate activity per day*) and where they can take part in cardiovascular activities. Monitor their own activity levels (*eg using diaries*) and compare this with the recommendations for young people.	4, 5	Posters, worksheets, activity diaries (*eg for 4 to 6 weeks*); notices, leaflets, internet PUPIL TASK CARD 2

EXAMPLE UNIT FOR INTEGRATING HRE WITHIN GAMES

Key Stage 3

Unit: HOCKEY
Year 7 or 8   Duration: 6-8 Hours

Objectives — To enable pupils to:
- Develop passing skills used in hockey.
- Develop attacking and defensive strategies in the game of hockey.
- Practise and develop knowledge of at least one team position.
- Establish independent warm-up and cool-down routines that are relevant to the game of hockey.
- Know where they can play hockey in the local community.

National Curriculum Links — Pupils should be taught:
Games: an invasion game, working from small-sided and modified versions to the recognised form; to develop the techniques, skills, strategies and tactics applicable to selected, recognised games; the rules, laws and scoring systems specific to selected games.
HRE: relevant and safe warm-up and cool-down routines, and how to take responsibility for their planning and execution; the range of activity opportunities at school, home and in the local community.

Learning Outcomes — Pupils should be able to:	Learning Activities — Opportunities for pupils to:	Assessment	Resources
1. Play at least one team position with understanding of rules and of specific role in attack and defence.	Experience and understand appropriate warm-up and cool-down activities which affect the heart rate, mobilise joints, stretch appropriate muscles, and are relevant to the game of hockey.	4	
2. Send the ball accurately to team members or score when appropriate.	Select activities which include numerous touches of the ball, limited opposition and changes in pace, and emphasise accuracy of the sending skills (*hitting, pushing*).	2	Ball between two or three players
3. Demonstrate understanding of how and when to provide support to team members.	Explore and practise (*in small-sided modified games*) principles of possession, invasion and scoring, on and off the ball (eg 3v1; 3v2; 3v3; 4v2;4v3;4v4;5v5), as appropriate to the experience and skill development of players.	1, 2, 3	Ball per group, grid
4. Plan and perform an appropriate warm-up and cool-down for hockey.	Make decisions about attacking play (*eg when to pass, when to shoot*) and defensive play (*eg when to tackle or intercept, how to regain possession*).	3	Goal, line/cones/target
5. Know where in the community they can play hockey.	Practise and refine pushing and hitting skills, varying the distance and speed, and avoiding opposition. Practise sympathetic passing to show awareness of others' limitations. Develop disguised passes to test opposition's strengths.	2	Bibs or bands
	Select a specific role to develop over time within a half or full game. Know the role requirements both in attack and in defence. Know the rules of hockey particularly as they apply to that position.	1, 3	
	Refine the sending skills required by the particular role they have selected (*eg shooting skills; hitting, pushing or kicking skills over short or long distances*).	2	
	Plan and perform own warm-up and cool-down relevant to the game of hockey.	4	PUPIL TASK CARD 4
	Discuss and find out where they can play more hockey at school and in the community.	5	Notices, leaflets, internet

Health Related Exercise — TEACHER'S HANDBOOK

PUPIL TASK CARD 1

Opportunity Knocks!

Topic: **Activity promotion**

Learning Outcomes

Pupils should
- Know the full range of activity opportunities and ways of incorporating exercise into everyday life
- Be able to access information about a wide range of activity opportunities.

National Curriculum Links

Pupils should be taught

Physical Education:
- The range of activity opportunities at school, home and in the local community, and ways of incorporating exercise into their lifestyles.

PSE:
- How to keep healthy, and be aware of influences on health
- That the balance between work, leisure and exercise affects mental health
- To recognise risk and make safer choices through gathering information relating to healthy and safe environments and lifestyles.

Equipment

Indoor and outdoor activity

Pupil Task Card 1 (*sufficient for use with individuals, groups or a whole class*)
Equipment for activities (*eg balls, bats, hoops, bean bags, cones*)

Theory

Other places where it is possible to be active might include: youth club, scouts/guides, community centre, village hall. There may be activities which pupils would like to try (*eg skate boarding*) but cannot because of lack of facilities, money, time, support and/or transport.

It is certainly not true that you can only be active regularly if you have money, access to transport and are good at sport. Different ways in which activity can be fitted into everyday life might include: helping in the garden; doing errands (*by foot or on a bike*); walking to meet friends; going for a jog; walking a dog; performing exercises (*eg skipping, curl ups*) in a room at home (*eg bedroom, garage*); doing a paper round, etc.

Information about the benefits of exercise and activity opportunities may be obtained from:
PE teachers, friends, local newspapers, school noticeboards, the internet, magazines, leaflets/pamphlets/brochures, coaches, parents, neighbours, noticeboards in libraries, sports clubs, leisure centres, health and fitness clubs, etc.

TEACHER'S HANDBOOK — Health Related Exercise

Practical

Pupils are to be involved in creating active games using limited equipment. They may find this difficult to start with, but provided that there are clear guidelines (*as on the card*) and they are not swamped with equipment (*a maximum of no more than one each of the following is recommended: bat, ball, hoop, bean bag and cone*), they should find, with time and thought, that they are able to invent 'new' activities or create variations of activities that they already know.

Pupils should be advised to keep the rules to a minimum initially (*in order for it to be safe and fair*) and to devise a simple scoring system (*if, indeed, one is required at all*) in order to avoid the activity becoming overly complex.

When evaluating the activities, pupils should be encouraged to be positive and constructive, and to state what they liked about the activity as well as what they think should be changed and how this could be done.

Groups should consider what they would include in specific warm-ups and cool-downs for their created activities.

Brain Teasers

- **'Lack of time' is one of the main reasons for not being more active. How can busy people fit activity into their life?**
  The easiest way may be to incorporate routine activity into everyday life so that it becomes a habit (*like brushing your teeth*). Examples include: walking or cycling to work or school instead of travelling by car or bus, using the stairs instead of the lift, being more active around the home and/or garden, dancing to music. It may also help to spend less time doing sedentary activities such as watching the TV, using the computer, listening to music, etc.

- **Can you think of any activities that require no equipment at all? What are the advantages of these activities?**
  Activities that require no equipment at all might include: walking, jogging, dancing, marching, jumping, astride jumps, curl ups, push ups, etc. The advantages of these types of activities is that they can be performed in numerous places and it is not necessary to have access to equipment or to be with a group of people in a particular place in order to be active.

- **Name a few exercises you could do if you were chair-bound due to an accident or injury. Why should you keep yourself active?**
  Bicep curls, shoulder raises, tricep exercises (*bending and straightening arm above head*), head turns and tilts, shoulder circles/shrugs/lifts, upper body twists, sidebends, etc. Depending on the nature of the accident/injury, it may also be possible to perform some or all of the following: wheelchair basketball, wheeling, wheelchair rugby, swimming, dancing, etc. It is important to keep active in order that the body systems (*eg cardiovascular, musculo-skeletal*) are working efficiently and health benefits (*physical, mental and social*) are maximised.

- **How many different sports can you name? Which ones would you like to try? Where can you find out more?**
  Sport England has a directory of all the different registered sports. This information is also on the internet. Keen pupils can be encouraged to access this information so that it can be made more readily available to pupils and staff. There may also be similar 'sport/exercise/physical activity' directories in local areas and regions.

Health Related Exercise — TEACHER'S HANDBOOK

PUPIL TASK CARD 2

Getting Personal

Topic | **Activity promotion**

Learning Outcomes

Pupils should
- Be active for 60 minutes per day (*in and out of school*); be aware of and able to monitor and evaluate personal activity levels over a period of time.

National Curriculum Links

Pupils should be taught

Physical Education:
- That appropriate training can improve fitness and performance.
- The range of activity opportunities at school, home and in the local community, and ways of incorporating exercise into their lifestyles.

PSE:
- To reflect on and assess their strengths in relation to personality, work and leisure and set realistic targets and review them.
- How to keep healthy, and be aware of influences on health.
- That the balance between work, leisure and exercise affects mental health.
- To recognise risk and make safer choices through gathering information relating to healthy and safe environments and lifestyles.

Equipment

Indoor and outdoor activity

Pupil Task Card 2 (*sufficient for use with individuals, groups or a whole class*)
Photocopies of simple activity plan (*see page 13 of this handbook*)

Theory

In order to answer the questions, pupils need to understand the difference between:
- Moderate intensity activity.
- Vigorous intensity activity.
- Strength exercise.
- Flexibility exercise.

Pupils also need to be encouraged to include what they do in PE lessons plus any activity that they do around the home and/or garden, and any active travelling (*eg walking or cycling*).

If pupils are attaining the recommended levels of activity for young people (*including strength and flexibility exercise*), they should be congratulated and encouraged to talk about where they are active and how they manage to fit activity into their lifestyles. Those pupils that are not reaching the recommended levels may need to become more aware of the activity opportunities at school and in the local community, and to consider ways in which they might be able to overcome obstacles or barriers to exercise (*eg not having enough time/money, etc*).

TEACHER'S HANDBOOK — **Health Related Exercise**

Practical

Designing an activity plan can take place in a PE lesson using the template below if required (*maybe using a 'wet weather' opportunity*) or be given as PE 'homework'. Alternatively it can be delivered as part of a PSE programme. If the card is used within a PE lesson, the pupils should be active and can start to follow their plan.

Examples of 'healthy' activities which might be added to the plan include: not eating cakes/sweets/biscuits/crisps; brushing teeth twice a day; drinking 2 glasses of water a day; not drinking fizzy, sugary drinks; being in bed by 10pm; watching no more than 2 hours TV a day, etc. It is important that pupils understand that 'being physically active' is one of a wide range of healthy behaviours.

Pupils should be encouraged to stick to their plan where possible (*including being active in and out of school*). If they are not able to adhere to their plan, they should note the reasons why (*eg feeling too tired, too much homework, no transport, etc*) so that these can be followed up and discussed at a later stage.

Activity	Mon	Tues	Wed	Thurs	Fri	Sat	Sun	Target	How did you do?
One hour of moderate and/or vigorous intensity activity								Daily	
Strength exercise								at least twice a week	
Flexibility exercise								at least twice a week	

Activity	Mon	Tues	Wed	Thurs	Fri	Sat	Sun	Target	How did you do?
One hour of moderate and/or vigorous intensity activity	cycle to school (20); swim (30)	cycle to school (20); football (40)	cycle to school (20); games lesson	cycle to school (20); walk (25)	cycle to school (20); dance lesson	walked to and from friend's house		Daily	Quite well - 6 out of 7 days; an hour on most days
Strength exercise	straight curl up (2x10)		twisting curl up (2x10)		movements in dance lesson	helped carry boxes at home		at least twice a week	very well - easily reached targets
Flexibility exercise			stretches in games lesson		stretches in dance lesson			at least twice a week	okay - just reached target

Brain Teasers

- **Targets should be specific, short-term and realistic. Were yours? Did you take on too much too soon? Was it too easy?**
  Target-setting is not always an easy task and it may be that targets set are too vague and beyond reach in the time available. Target-setting should improve with practice. Precise and manageable targets which represent progress from the baseline (*eg going swimming once a week*) are to be encouraged. Remember that exercise does not have to hurt to be healthy.

- **Some exercise is better than none - even 10 minutes worth is better than nothing. Why is this?**
  Being active is healthier than being inactive. Physical, mental and social health benefits are to be gained from even moderate amounts of activity. The benefits of short amounts of exercise accumulate over time. Be aware that the 60 minutes of recommended activity time for young people can be accumulated over the day (*eg 1 x 60; 2 x 30; 3 x 20; 4 x 15; 6 x 10 minutes*).

- **Do you think it possible to overdo exercise? What problems could this cause? How can this be avoided?**
  Yes, it is possible to overdo exercise. A small proportion of individuals may even become obsessed with being active and may be over-exercising or over-training (*eg training 3 to 4 hours a day with no rest days*). This can cause serious problems such as fatigue, exhaustion, illness, digestive problems, severe weightloss, dehydration, social exclusion, etc. This can be avoided by adopting a sensible, common-sense approach to being active. Following the recommended amounts for young people will help to maximise the benefits of activity and minimise any risks involved.

- **Rewarding yourself can help to keep you going. Can you think of any 'healthy' rewards?**
  'Healthy' rewards might include: having a piece of fruit; going to the cinema; buying a record or CD or magazine or book; buying an item which can be used for activity (*eg pair of sports socks/shorts, skipping rope, etc*); attending an activity class (*eg aerobics, step, circuits*); going to see some live sport (*eg hockey/netball/football/rugby match*).

- **Why do we tend to give up when things go wrong (*eg breaking a new year's resolution*) What should we do instead?**
  Sticking to a resolution can be hard work - it requires self-discipline and a belief in yourself and in the benefits involved. Once we have broken a resolution (*eg eating a biscuit on the last day of January*), the easiest option is to forget the resolution (*ie giving up biscuits*) and return to previous habits. What we should do instead is to applaud ourselves for keeping the resolution for as long as we did (*30 days without biscuits is good going!*) and to re-start as soon as we feel capable of doing so.

PUPIL TASK CARD 3

BRAINTEASERS

Getting Going and Getting Over It

LEARNING OUTCOMES

NATIONAL CURRICULUM LINKS

EQUIPMENT

THEORY

PRACTICAL

Topic Preparation for and recovery from physical activity

Learning Outcomes
Pupils should
- Know and understand the value of preparing for and recovering from activity and the purpose of each of the components of a warm-up and a cool-down.
- Be able to plan and perform parts of a warm-up and a cool-down.

National Curriculum Links
Pupils should be taught

Physical Education:
- Relevant and safe warm-up and cool-down routines (*eg mobility exercises, whole-body activities and static stretches*) and how to take responsibility for their planning and execution.

PSE:
- To recognise risk and make safer choices through gathering information relating to healthy and safe environments and lifestyles.

Equipment
Indoor and outdoor activity

Pupil Task Card 3 (*sufficient for use with individuals, groups or a whole class*)
Equipment relating to main activity of lesson (*eg balls, bats/sticks*) (*optional*)

Theory

Two additional reasons for warming up:
- To PREVENT injury
- To improve PERFORMANCE

Three main parts to a warm-up:
- CARDIOVASCULAR activities
- MOBILITY or MOBILISING exercises
- FLEXIBILITY exercises

Three reasons for cooling down:
- To help your mind and body recover from the exertion
- To help distribute waste products from the muscles
- To help prevent or lessen muscular stiffness and soreness

Types of activity involved in cooling down:
- PULSE LOWERING activities
- FLEXIBILITY exercises

TEACHER'S HANDBOOK **Health Related Exercise**

Practical

Activities to gradually increase heart rate and breathing might include: walking, jogging, running, sidestepping, skipping, galloping, low jumping, criss-crossing feet, marching, knee lifts, dribbling or bouncing a ball, etc. The activity should involve movement of the legs as these are the largest muscles in the body. It should not involve racing, sprinting or any fast, jerky movements.

Exercises for joints might include: shoulder circles, arm circles, knee bends, knee lifts, marching, raising up onto toes, head turns (*left and right*), head circling (*around front only*), side bends (*with hands on waist/hips to support back*), upper body twists (*with hips and knees facing forward*). Each exercise should be performed with good technique - not necessarily slowly but under control and without flinging.

Appropriate stretches might include: calf and quadriceps muscles (*for running and jumping activities*), hamstrings (*for kicking and bending activities*), adductors or groin muscles (*for sideways and lunging activities*), pectorals, triceps and deltoids (*for throwing, catching and lifting activities*). All stretches should be moved into slowly and held still for 6-10 seconds. Pupils should know where in the body the stretch is and they should start to learn the names of the muscles.

The main activity could be cross-country running, skipping, exercise to music, etc or a lively activity from an appropriate area of activity.

Activities to gradually decrease the heart rate and slow down breathing might include any of those suggested for the pulse-raising part of the warm-up. They should involve movement of the legs but no racing, sprinting or fast, jerky movements.

Appropriate stretches might include any of those suggested for the warm-up and can be held for longer.

Brain Teasers

- **Why should stretches be held still?**
  Bouncing in stretches can cause muscle tears at the ends of the muscle and, long-term, can result in decreased flexibility around joints due to the presence of scar tissue. The most important stretches are those for the major muscle groups in the legs (*calf muscles, quadriceps, hamstrings*), groin (*adductors*), upper body (*pectorals, triceps, deltoids*), back (*trapezius, erector spinae*) and abdominals (*obliques, rectus abdominis*).

- **Why have the stretches been left until last?**
  The safest time to lengthen muscle fibres is when they are warm because this is when they are more elastic and pliable.

- **Why can stretches in the cool-down be held for longer than those in the warm-up?**
  Following energetic activity, the muscles are very warm and, as a result, more elastic and pliable. The cool-down is, therefore, a particularly safe and effective time to hold the muscles in a lengthened position for longer.

- **Think of activities or exercises which you should avoid doing in a warm-up. Can you explain why?**
  The following should be avoided: any racing activities (*eg relays*), bouncing stretches, problem exercises (*eg standing toe touches, full head circling*), strength exercises (*eg curl ups*), and exercises which place your joints (*eg neck, back, knees*) in awkward positions or cause pain. All of these have the potential to cause discomfort and injury (*eg strains, sprains*).

- **How many 'whole body' exercises that do not need equipment can you name? Why are these useful for warm-ups and cool-downs?**
  Walking, jogging, running, sidestepping, skipping, galloping, low jumping, criss-crossing feet, marching, knee lifts, etc. They can be performed in any indoor or outdoor space and are not reliant on equipment being available. This is particularly useful with large numbers and/or limited resources.

- **A hot bath is often advised after a tiring game or performance. How can this help your body to recover?**
  The hot water dilates the blood vessels which promotes and increases the circulation of blood to and from the muscles. This assists in bringing additional nutrients to the muscles and removing waste products, thus helping the muscles to recover and repair.

PUPIL TASK CARD 4

Getting Down to Specifics

Topic: Preparation for and recovery from physical activity

Learning Outcomes

Pupils should
- Be able to plan and perform a safe relevant warm-up and cool-down for general activity and for a specific activity.

National Curriculum Links

Pupils should be taught

Physical Education:
- Relevant and safe warm-up and cool-down routines (*eg mobility exercises, whole-body activities and static stretches*) and how to take responsibility for their planning and execution.

PSE:
- To recognise risk and make safer choices through gathering information relating to healthy and safe environments and lifestyles.

Equipment

Indoor and outdoor activity

Pupil Task Card 4 (*sufficient for use with individuals, groups or a whole class*)
Equipment relating to main activity(ies) of lesson (*eg balls, bats/sticks*)

Theory

A good cool-down should:
- Help your mind and body recover from the exertion, distribute waste products from the muscles, and prevent or lessen muscular stiffness and soreness.
- Include exercises which are safe to perform and are sensible for your age, physique and activity level.

A general warm-up for games should include:
- CARDIOVASCULAR activities; examples: walking, jogging, running, sidestepping, skipping, galloping, low jumping, criss-crossing feet, marching, knee lifts, etc.
- MOBILITY or MOBILISING exercises; examples: shoulder circles, arm circles, knee bends, knee lifts, marching, raising up onto toes, head turns, head circling, side bends, upper body twists, etc.
- FLEXIBILITY exercises; examples: stretches for calf and quadriceps muscles, hamstrings, adductors or groin muscles, pectorals, triceps and deltoids.

A general cool-down for games should include:
- PULSE LOWERING activities; examples: walking, jogging, running, sidestepping, knee lifts, etc.
- FLEXIBILITY exercises; examples: stretches for calf and quadriceps muscles, hamstrings, adductors or groin muscles, pectorals, triceps and deltoids.

Teacher's Handbook — Health Related Exercise

Practical

Activities to gradually increase heart rate and breathing should involve movement of the leg muscles. Examples: walking, jogging, running, sidestepping, skipping, knee lifts, dribbling or bouncing a ball, moving to get to or catch a ball, etc. Discourage racing or fast, jerky movements.

Examples of exercises for joints: shoulder circles and/or arm circles (for *throwing, catching, reaching activities*), knee bends, knee lifts and/or marching (for *running, jumping, kicking, bending activities*), head turns (*left and right*) and/or head circling (*around front only*) (for *quick head movements, changes of direction*), side bends (*with hands on waist/hips to support back*) and/or upper body twists (*with hips and knees facing forward*) (for *sideways, lunging, lifting, carrying, pulling, pushing activities*). All should be performed with control and without flinging.

Examples of appropriate stretches: calf and quadriceps muscles (for *running, jumping activities*), hamstrings (for *kicking, bending activities*), adductors or groin muscles (for *sideways, lunging activities*), pectorals, triceps and deltoids (for *throwing, catching, lifting activities*). The stretches should be held still for 6-10 seconds.

The main activity could be the same for all or pupils could select from options.

Examples of activities to gradually decrease the heart rate and slow down breathing include any of those suggested for the pulse-raising part of the warm-up but they should be performed at a slower rate.

Examples of appropriate stretches include any of those suggested for the warm-up and can be held for 10-20 seconds. This is longer than in the warm-up because, following energetic activity, the muscles are warm, more elastic and pliable, and can safely and effectively be held in a lengthened position for more time. Pupils can check their technique by: (i) being observed and, where necessary, corrected by the teacher and/or any non-participants, (ii) watching and helping each other (*eg in pairs or small groups*), (iii) checking their technique against illustrations on a worksheet or poster.

Brain Teasers

- **Why is a specific warm-up or cool-down usually more effective than a general one?**
  A specific warm-up or cool-down includes cardiovascular activities, mobility exercises and stretches which are 'tailor made' to the activity. This can be more effective than a general warm-up in preparing the mind and body for the actions and movements associated with that particular activity.

- **How many whole body movements that you could use in a warm-up for gymnastics or dance can you name?**
  Travelling on feet in a variety of ways (*eg small steps, large strides, hopping, galloping, skipping, turning body, etc*); travelling on various parts of feet (*eg toes*); bending legs, low jumping, etc.

- **What would you expect the main differences to be between a warm-up for a 100m sprint and one for javelin throwing?**
  The sprint warm-up should focus predominantly on gradually increasing the intensity of the cardiovascular activities (*from a slow jog to faster running*), mobilising the joints in the lower body (*ankles, knees, hips*) and stretches for muscles in the lower body; the javelin warm-up should focus predominantly on cardiovascular activities to warm the muscles, mobility exercises for the hips, back, shoulders, elbows and fingers, and stretches for muscles in the chest, back, shoulders and arms.

- **What do top-level tennis or football players include in their warm-up? Why do we know less about how they cool-down?**
  Cardiovascular activities (*with and without equipment*), mobility exercises and stretches related to their sport. Examples: jogging, running, lunging, side bends, arm circles, hamstring stretch, adductors or groin stretch. We know less about the cool-down, particularly the stretches, as these may be performed inside in the changing rooms or following a hot shower or bath.

- **Flexibility is sometimes considered to be the 'forgotten' component of fitness. Why do you think this is?**
  Much attention is usually paid to cardiovascular and strength work and flexibility is often overlooked. This is unfortunate as muscles need to be both strong and supple in order for them to perform at their best and avoid unnecessary injury. Strong, tight muscles (*eg hamstrings in footballers*) are prone to strains which are painful and frustrating due to having to stop playing for a period of time.

PUPIL TASK CARD 5

The Highs and Lows of Exercise

Topic: Cardiovascular health

Learning Outcomes
Pupils should
- Be able to plan and perform safe, effective and developmentally-appropriate cardiovascular exercises of varying intensities and impacts.

National Curriculum Links
Pupils should be taught

Physical Education:
- To monitor a range of short-term effects on the cardiovascular system.

PSE:
- To recognise risk and make safer choices through gathering information relating to healthy and safe environments and lifestyles.

Equipment
Indoor and outdoor activity

Pupil Task Card 5 (*sufficient for use with individuals, groups or a whole class*)
Equipment relating to main activity(ies) of lesson (*eg skipping ropes, benches, cones*)

Theory

Common reasons for being active include:
- Having fun
- Staying healthy
- Being with friends
- Getting out of the house
- Getting fit
- Enjoying winning

Cardiovascular exercises: walking, jogging, running, swimming, sidestepping, skipping, galloping, jumping, marching, knee lifts, playing active games, aerobics, dancing, etc.

Examples of high intensity (*or vigorous*) exercise: race walking, sprinting, long jumping, skipping, bounding, astride jumps, shuttle running, energetic games playing, fast swimming, fast cycling, lively dancing. These cannot usually be performed for long as they are particularly tiring and the body cannot take in enough oxygen to work at such a fast pace over a period of time (*high intensity exercise is predominantly anaerobic*).

Examples of low intensity (*or light*) exercise: strolling, very easy jogging, slow swimming, bowls, golf, slow cycling. These can be performed for a long time as they are not very tiring and the body can easily take in enough oxygen to continue working over a period of time.

Moderate intensity exercise involves getting slightly out of breath and feeling warm (*it is more demanding than light exercise and less demanding than vigorous exercise*). Examples of moderate intensity exercise: brisk walking, easy jogging, steady swimming, dancing, games playing, steady cycling. Moderate intensity exercises are particularly beneficial as they can be performed for a reasonable time (*eg at least 10-15 minutes*), do not involve exhausting work, and are linked with health benefits. Examples of high impact exercise: bounding, vaulting, long jump, astride jumps, any exercise which involves jumping, fast bench stepping (*running up and down bench*). Examples of low impact exercise: cycling, knee lifts (*without jumping*), side-steps, marching (*without pounding feet*), bench stepping. Examples of energetic low-impact exercise: large side-steps, high knee lifts (*knee up towards chest*), large step-backs.

TEACHER'S HANDBOOK — Health Related Exercise

Practical

Light to moderate intensity activities which feel easy to perform and increase heart rate and breathing include: walking, jogging, running, side-stepping, skipping, knee lifts, dribbling or bouncing a ball, moving to get to or catch a ball, etc. These represent the pulse-raising part of the warm-up.

Examples of exercises for joints: shoulder circles and/or arm circles, knee bends, knee lifts and/or marching, head turns (*left and right*) and/or head circling (*around front only*), side bends (*with hands on waist/hips to support back*) and/or upper body twists (*with hips and knees facing forward*). Examples of appropriate stretches: calf and quadriceps muscles, hamstrings, adductors or groin muscles, pectorals, triceps and deltoids.

Example circuit of moderate to vigorous activities: bench stepping (*low impact*), tuck jumps (*high impact*), astride jumps (*high impact*), marching (*low impact*), knee lifts (*low impact*), skipping (*high impact*).

Cool-down: examples of moderate to light intensity activities and appropriate stretches include any of those suggested for the warm-up.

Brain Teasers

- **Why is it sensible to mix impacts and intensities in a circuit?**
  Mixing impacts and intensities helps to ensure that participants are able to complete a sequence of exercises within a circuit without becoming unnecessarily exhausted (*which might occur if a series of high intensity exercises were performed*) and without putting undue stress on the joints (*which might occur if a series of high impact exercises were performed*).

- **If you are not fit and do little exercise, which activity is best for you - low, moderate or high intensity. Low or high impact?**
  Low and/or moderate intensity exercise is most suitable for low fit, low active individuals. This feels more comfortable and enjoyable, and can be continued for longer. Low impact exercise is also particularly suitable for low fit, low active individuals as it does not place undue stress on their joints.

- **Do you know which intensity activity adults and young people are encouraged to do?**
  Adults and young people are encouraged to do at least moderate intensity activity as both moderate intensity and vigorous intensity exercise are associated with health benefits (*eg reduced risk of heart disease*).

- **Most games are a mixture of 'highs' and 'lows'. What is meant by this?**
  Games playing can be described as having physical 'highs' and 'lows' as it usually involves both high and low intensity and high and low impact exercise. In addition, games playing can be said to involve mental 'highs' and 'lows' as it usually results in either winning or losing.

PUPIL TASK CARD 6

Healthy Heart Happenings

Topic: Cardiovascular health

Learning Outcomes

Pupils should
- Understand and be able to monitor a range of effects of cardiovascular exercise
- Understand the range of effects of cardiovascular exercise on physical, mental and social health.

National Curriculum Links

Pupils should be taught

Physical Education:
- To monitor a range of short-term effects on the cardiovascular system.
- The long-term effects of exercise on physical health.
- The value of exercise to social and psychological well-being.

PSE:
- How to keep healthy, and be aware of influences on health.
- That the balance between work, leisure and exercise affects mental health.
- To recognise risk and make safer choices through gathering information relating to healthy and safe environments and lifestyles.

Equipment

Indoor and outdoor activity

Pupil Task Card 6 (*sufficient for use with individuals, groups or a whole class*)
Equipment relating to a range of cardiovascular activities (*eg skipping ropes, benches, basketballs*)

Theory

Cardiovascular exercise can also be referred to as:
- CARDIO-RESPIRATORY exercise
- STAMINA or ENDURANCE exercise
- AEROBIC exercise

Effects and Explanations:
- Heart rate increases — To pump blood around body more quickly
- Appearance might change — Due to blood vessels dilating and coming closer to skin surface (*looking flushed*) to help regulate body temperature
- Body temperature increases — Due to muscles producing heat when they work

Over time, fitness increases due to the cardiovascular system becoming more efficient, and performance improves due to increased practice and being able to work for longer before tiring. The processes involved (*eg increasing the number of blood vessels within the heart and the amount of blood pumped out*) take time to develop.

Separating out the effects on physical, social and mental health is difficult but the following are possible answers. Physical health: improved working of circulatory and respiratory systems; reduced risk of heart disease and obesity. Mental and social health: reduced risk of depression, anxiety, stress, and increased feelings of well-being, self-esteem, confidence. Physical, mental and social health: improved ability to manage conditions (*eg asthma, diabetes*); improved fitness for life and for sport.

TEACHER'S HANDBOOK — Health Related Exercise

Practical

Walking quickly or jogging easily should cause the heart rate, breathing rate and body temperature to increase. In addition, appearance may change (*eg individual becoming flushed*). The exercise should feel reasonably comfortable to perform.

Mobility exercises for the hips: knee lifts, marching, hip circling (*keeping knees still*). Mobility exercises for the spine: head turns (*left and right*) and/or head circling (*around front only*), side bends (*with hands on waist/hips to support back*) and/or upper body twists (*with hips and knees facing forward*). Mobility exercises for the shoulders: shoulder circles and/or arm circles (*forwards, backwards; one side at a time, both sides together*), shoulder lifts, shoulder shrugs.

Performing a range of cardiovascular exercises should cause the heart rate, breathing rate and body temperature to rapidly increase, appearance to change (*eg flushed, hot-looking face*) and feelings to vary, depending on the activity, from comfortable and enjoyable to very tiring.

Following energetic activity, walking quickly or jogging easily should cause the heart rate, breathing rate and body temperature to decrease, appearance to start returning to normal, and feelings to change (*eg exercise feeling comfortable to perform*).

Following the stretches, recovery from the exercise can be detected in terms of the heart and breathing rate returning towards pre-exercise rates, the body feeling and looking less hot, appearance returning to normal, and feeling tired but comfortable.

Brain Teasers

- **Many young people are active because it is fun, they can take part with their friends and it keeps them fit. Do you agree with this? Can you think of other reasons?**
  Other reasons for being active might include: being healthy; getting out of the house; wanting to take part; enjoying winning/competition; liking a challenge.

- **Some young people do not like exercise. Why do you think this is? Have you any ideas for encouraging them to be more active?**
  They may not like exercise because: it can hurt and may be painful; it can be humiliating; you have to wear certain clothes; it is expensive; it takes time; they do not think they are any good at it; they have not enjoyed previous experiences; it involves getting sweaty, having showers, etc. Ideas for encouraging them to be more active might include: being given more choice about the activities; having more and/or different activities on offer; having different types of groups for PE/sport/exercise; changing some of the regulations regarding showers and kit; improving the shower area; setting up a staff-student exercise committee, etc.

- **Some exercise effects are common to everyone but there are also individual differences. Why do you think this is?**
  When people exercise, similar effects occur (*eg heart rate, breathing rate and body temperature increase*). However, there will always be some element of individual difference because each person is different in terms of their size, shape and physique and also with respect to their state of health and their activity and fitness levels.

- **Brisk walking, jogging and cycling are healthy forms of exercise but some people do not enjoy them. Suggest ways of making them more interesting and think of alternative activities?**
  Walking, jogging and cycling may be made more interesting by: varying the areas and routes; taking part with someone else or a group of people (*eg joining a club*); introducing fun ideas such as a trim trail, treasure hunt; trying a variation of the activity eg orienteering, hill-walking, rambling, touring. Alternatives include: swimming, skipping, dancing, aerobics, roller-blading.

PUPIL TASK CARD 7

Major Muscle Movements

Topic: **Musculo-skeletal health**

Learning Outcomes

Pupils should
- Be able to plan and perform safe, effective and developmentally-appropriate musculo-skeletal exercises for the major muscle groups.

National Curriculum Links

Pupils should be taught

Physical Education:
- To monitor a range of short-term effects on the musculo-skeletal system.
- To adopt good posture when sitting, standing and taking part in activity.

PSE:
- To recognise risk and make safer choices through gathering information relating to healthy and safe environments and lifestyles.

Equipment

Indoor activity

Pupil Task Card 7 (*sufficient for use with individuals, groups or a whole class*)
Mats, music (*about 120 bpm with a strong steady beat*) (*optional*)

Theory

Large muscles in the body:
- CALF muscles — back part of your lower leg
- QUADRICEP muscles — front part of your upper leg
- HAMSTRING muscles — back part of your upper leg
- TRICEP muscles — back part of your upper arm
- GROIN muscles — inside of your upper leg
- PECTORAL muscles — chest

Muscles are attached to BONES and they PULL on them to make them move;
Muscles are attached to bones by tough TENDONS;
Bones meet at a JOINT; different types: hinge, ball and socket, gliding;
There are LIGAMENTS at joints to help the bones move in the correct directions;
Muscles contain lots of fibres which shorten or CONTRACT when they work.

Cardiovascular exercises: walking, jogging, swimming, dancing, cycling, games playing (*eg basketball, badminton, tennis, netball, hockey, football, rugby, etc*), exercise activities (*eg astride jumps, bench stepping, knee lifts, side-stepping, marching, etc*).

Large muscles in the legs and arms get some exercise through everyday activities (*eg walking, using stairs, lifting, carrying*). However, muscles in the trunk region (*middle part of the body*) such as the abdominals and the back muscles are often neglected.

The muscles in the stomach and back bring about movement of the vertebrae in the SPINE. Good posture involves standing/sitting tall, head forward, shoulders back, stomach firm, backside in. Good posture results in less stress on the spine and reduced risk of back pain.

Practical

The warm-up could include any cardiovascular activity (*eg walking, jogging, skipping, marching*). It should also include joint exercises for the shoulders (*eg circles, lifts, shrugs*) and the middle and lower part of the spine (*eg hip circling - keeping knees still*), side bends (*with hands on waist/hips to support back*), upper body twists (*with hips and knees facing forward*)). Stretches should be included for the muscles in the trunk region (*eg reaching up tall and long; reaching to one side (with one hand on hip to help support spine); hands on thighs, curving back towards ceiling; linking hands/wrists in front of body and rounding upper back*)).

- Straight curl ups   1: hands on floor; 2: hands on thighs; 3: hands at side of head.
- Back raises   1: hands at side; 2: hands near head; hands out sideways.
- Twisting curl ups   1: hand to knee; 2: shoulder towards knee; 3: shoulder to knee.
- Shoulder squeezes   1: sitting; 2: lying, hands at side; 3: lying, hands near head.

The numbers represent different versions of the exercise, 1 being the easiest. Exercise technique can be checked: (i) by being observed and, where necessary, corrected (*teacher, non-participants*), (ii) by watching and helping each other (*eg pairs, groups*), (iii) against illustrations on a worksheet or poster. Exercises for the stomach and back muscles have been alternated to avoid these muscles becoming over-fatigued. The common theme is that all the exercises improve postural muscles.

The following stretches should be performed: rectus abdominis (*standing or lying, reaching long and tall*); erector spinae (*curving back as in cat stretch on all fours or from sitting*); obliques (*lying on back, both knees bent to one side, head turned away from knees*); trapezius (*linking hands infront and rounding upper back*).

Brain Teasers

● **Which muscles support the spine? Name exercises which work these muscles. Why should they be performed regularly?**

The main muscles supporting the spine are: rectus abdominis, obliques, erector spinae, trapezius, and gluteus maximus (*backside muscle*). Exercises which work these muscles are: straight and twisting curl ups, back raises, shoulder squeezes and leg raises. These exercises should be performed regularly as they help keep the muscles toned, improve posture and reduce the risk of back pain.

● **There are 10-12 major muscle groups in the body. What are they? Find them on a muscle poster.**

The major muscle groups in the body are in the legs (*calf and shin muscles, hamstrings, quadriceps*), the pelvic region (*inner thigh/groin - adductors, outer thigh - abductors, gluteus maximus*), the trunk (*rectus abdominis, obliques, erector spinae*), and the upper body (*trapezius, pectorals, triceps, biceps*).

● **Describe what is meant by good technique for lifting, carrying, placing and using equipment.**

Good technique involves: getting close to the object being lifted; keeping a wide, solid base with feet apart and firmly on the ground; using the large leg muscles rather than the back muscles; tightening the tummy muscles; keeping the back straight when lifting or lowering; holding the object close to the body; and getting assistance if the object is very heavy.

● **The right sort of training can improve your fitness and performance. Explain why this is.**

The most effective way of improving fitness and performance for a particular sport or activity is to ensure that the training includes exercises which work on the specific energy systems (*aerobic or anaerobic or both*), and the specific muscles, joints and bones used in the sport or activity.

● **Back pain is the most common medical complaint in Great Britain. Why do you think this is?**

Back pain is often caused by poor postural habits (*eg slouching, rounded shoulders, protruding stomach, arched back*), inefficient lifting and carrying techniques (*eg using back muscles rather than legs, twisting the back*), lack of exercise (*particularly for the postural muscles*), and/or excess body weight.

PUPIL TASK CARD 8

Muscling in on Your Health

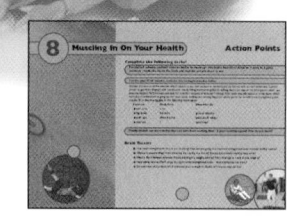

Topic: Musculo-skeletal health

Learning Outcomes

Pupils should

- Understand and be able to monitor a range of effects of musculo-skeletal exercise; understand the range of effects of musculo-skeletal exercise on physical, mental and social health.

National Curriculum Links

Pupils should be taught

Physical Education:

- To monitor a range of short-term effects on the musculo-skeletal system.
- The long-term effects of exercise on physical health.
- The value of exercise to social and psychological well-being.

PSE:
- How to keep healthy, and be aware of influences on health.
- That the balance between work, leisure and exercise affects mental health.
- To recognise risk and make safer choices through gathering information relating to healthy and safe environments and lifestyles.

Equipment

Indoor activity

Pupil Task Card 8 (*sufficient for use with individuals, groups or a whole class*)
Mats, music (*about 120 bpm with a strong steady beat*) (*optional*)

Theory

Working muscles against a force or resistance is called:
- STRENGTH exercise
- ENDURANCE exercise
- MUSCULO-SKELETAL exercise

You also need to perform STRETCH exercises for muscles that have worked hard in order to keep them supple and flexible. If this is not done, the muscles may become short and tight and this will have an adverse effect on performance (*eg not being able to reach, throw or kick as far*).

Muscular strength and endurance increases due to the muscle fibres becoming larger and increasing in number; muscle tone and posture improve due to the muscles being exercised and becoming firmer and stronger; flexibility increases providing that the muscles which have been worked are frequently and safely lengthened; performance improves due to increased practice and being able to work harder and for longer before tiring. The complex processes involved (*eg fibres increasing*) take time.

Separating out the effects on physical, social and mental health is difficult but the following are possible answers. Physical health: improved working of muscles, bones and joints; reduced risk of back pain, bone disease, osteoporosis. Mental and social health: reduced risk of depression, anxiety, stress, and increased feelings of well-being, self-esteem, confidence. Physical, mental and social health: improved ability to manage conditions (*eg arthritis, stiff joints*); improved fitness for life and for sport.

Practical

The warm-up can include any cardiovascular activity. It should also include joint exercises for the shoulders, and the middle and lower part of the spine, and stretches for the muscles in the trunk region.

- Arm curls   1: light dumbell; 2: moderate dumbell; 3: heavier dumbell.
- Leg raises   1: from lying on front; all fours, low leg: all fours, higher leg.
- Push ups   1: from all fours; 2: three-quarter position; 3: full length.
- Step ups   1: low step; 2: moderate step; 3: higher step.

The numbers represent different versions of the exercise, 1 being the easiest.

Missing gaps in information on cards: biceps; legs.

Exercise technique can be checked: (i) by being observed and, where necessary, corrected (*teacher, non-participants*), (ii) by watching and helping each other (*eg pairs, groups*), (iii) against illustrations on a worksheet or poster.

Brain Teasers

● **How much strength work should you be doing? How are you going to incorporate strength exercises into your weekly routine?**
Young people should be doing strength exercise at least twice a week. This can take the form of a range of weight-bearing activities such as gymnastics, dancing, aerobics, climbing, skipping, jumping events, sports (*eg basketball*) and/or structured exercise (*eg body conditioning or resistance exercises*).

● **What is circuit-training? What exercises are usually in a circuit? Do you know which muscles they work?**
Circuit-training involves performing a series of exercises in a set sequence. Exercises which are usually in a circuit include: straight and twisting curl ups (*rectus abdominis and obliques*), push ups (*pectorals and triceps*), arm curls (*biceps*), bench stepping (*quadriceps and calf muscles*), astride jumps (*quadriceps, calf muscles, abductors and adductors*) and pull ups (*biceps*).

● **What is the difference between circuit-training and weight-training? From what age is it safe to use weights?**
Weight-training involves the use of external weights such as barbells and fixed weight machines. Circuit-training usually involves body weight exercises and occasionally the use of low resistance material (*eg elastics, light dumbells*). It is only safe to use heavy external weights once the body has stopped growing. As a general rule, key stage four and five pupils (*aged 14 years+*) can use light to moderate resistance material (*eg elastics, dumbells, fixed machines*) provided that they are lifting weights that they can comfortably cope with, and that they perform the exercises with good technique.

● **Many adults cannot afford to go to a gym to do strength exercises. What alternatives are there?**
The alternatives are to perform exercises at home (*eg curl ups in the bedroom; work-out in the garage*) and/or to follow exercise videos.

PUPIL TASK CARD 9

Performing a Balancing Act

Topic: Energy balance

Learning Outcomes

Pupils should
- Know and understand that whole body activities help to reduce body fat, and conditioning exercises help to tone muscles.
- Know and understand that increasing activity levels and eating a balanced diet can help to maintain a healthy body weight.
- Know and understand that the body needs a minimum daily energy intake in order to function properly, and that strict dieting and excessive exercising can damage one's health.
- Be able to perform safe, effective and developmentally-appropriate cardiovascular and musculo-skeletal exercises appropriate for maintaining a healthy body weight.

National Curriculum Links

Pupils should be taught

Physical Education:
- The long-term effects of exercise on physical health.
- The differences between whole-body activities that help to reduce body fat and conditioning exercises that improve muscle tone.
- The value of exercise to social and psychological well-being.

PSE:
- How to keep healthy, and be aware of influences on health.
- That the balance between work, leisure and exercise affects mental health.
- To recognise risk and make safer choices through gathering information relating to healthy and safe environments and lifestyles.

Equipment

Indoor activity

Pupil Task Card 9 (sufficient for use with individuals, groups or a whole class)
Mats, equipment for activities (eg skipping ropes), music (optional).

Theory

If you eat and drink a lot and do very little activity, you are likely to:
- GAIN weight in the form of body fat.

If you reduce the calories you take in and do more activity, you are likely to:
- LOSE weight in the form of body fat.

It is better to adopt a long-term weight management plan than go on a quick fix weight-loss diet because the latter can result in fatigue, illness, and weight reduction due to loss of water rather than body fat. Crash dieting and over-exercising are not good for your health because they are extreme behaviours which can create problems such as digestive disorders, exhaustion, dehydration and over use injuries.

The following five statements represent good advice:
- Eat more fruit and vegetables.
- Use the stairs instead of the lift.
- Try and do some activity every day.
- Eat more pasta, potatoes, bread.
- Drink more water.

Practical

Activities to warm the body that do not include walking, jogging or running are: skipping, side-stepping, galloping, criss-crossing feet, hopping, knee lifts, marching, etc.

The cardiovascular activities (*brisk walking, jogging, stepping, aerobics or dance moves, side-stepping or galloping, skipping, astride jumps*) are whole body activities involving large muscle groups which use up many calories and help to reduce body fat. The strength exercises (*straight and twisting curl ups*) help to tone the muscles in the abdominal region.

Muscles which are often 'tight' are the pectorals (*especially in individuals with rounded shoulders*), triceps, groin or adductors, hip flexors (*muscle which runs from top of leg to lower back*) and the hamstrings.

A sensible order involves mixing intensities and impacts to ensure that you can keep exercising for 15-20 minutes without exhausting yourself or putting too much pressure on your joints.

Brain Teasers

- **The body needs a minimum daily energy intake to function properly. What is the intake? For what functions is it needed?**
  Growing bodies require about 1500 calories per day in order to carry out essential functions relating to breathing, digestion, growth and development.

- **It is estimated that about 10-20% of young people are very overweight. What do you think are the main reasons for this?**
  The main reasons are considered to relate to sedentary lifestyles (*eg excessive TV/video watching, computer use, eating lots of fast food, being transported from place to place, doing little exercise, etc*).

- **What simple methods are there of keeping a check on your weight? What ways are there of increasing your activity levels?**
  Simple methods include using weighing scales, taking girth measurements (*eg around waist, hips*), trying on clothes of a particular size, taking a good look at yourself in the mirror. Activity levels can be increased by: walking or cycling to school/shops/meet friends, using stairs instead of lifts, being more active around the home and garden, doing more exercise, joining a sports club, etc.

- **More adults are becoming overweight. Why is this? There are Government targets to reduce obesity. Why do you think this is?**
  Adults are becoming overweight for the same reasons that young people are: sedentary living (*eg excessive TV/video watching, computer use, fast food, driving/taking buses, doing little exercise, etc*). The Government has set targets as it is worried about the increase in ill-health associated with rising obesity figures and the cost of this to the National Health Service.

- **Anorexia nervosa and bulimia are eating disorders. How can you control your weight and avoid these disorders?**
  These disorders can be avoided by adopting a sensible long-term approach to managing weight. It is dangerous to adopt extreme behaviours (*such as eating tiny amounts of food or causing your body to reject food*) as it results in lack of energy, fatigue, exhaustion, dehydration, digestive disorders, anti-social behaviour, etc. There is no need to lose weight for cosmetic reasons - individuals should learn to like and respect their bodies - they should not aim to look like thin models or pop stars - these people are not necessarily healthy, happy or contented.

Health Related Exercise — TEACHER'S HANDBOOK

PUPIL TASK CARD 10

Maximising the Benefits and - Minimising the Risks

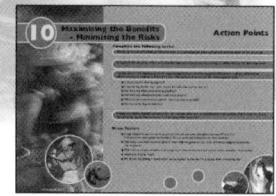

Topic: Safety

Learning Outcomes

Pupils should
- Know how to maximise the health benefits of physical activity; be aware of any risks involved and know how to minimise them.

National Curriculum Links

Pupils should be taught

Physical Education:
- To adopt safe practices and procedures when taking part in physical activities that might require the wearing of protective clothing, the removal of jewellery to avoid injury, the supervised use of equipment or response to specific weather conditions.

PSE:
- How to keep healthy, and be aware of influences on health.
- To recognise risk and make safer choices through gathering information relating to healthy and safe environments and lifestyles.

Equipment

Indoor or outdoor activity

Pupil Task Card 10 (*sufficient for use with individuals, groups or a whole class*)
Equipment for activities

Theory

It may be that, despite the benefits, some people do little or no exercise because: they do not know or understand the benefits; they have not enjoyed previous exercise experiences; they do not know about activity opportunities in their area or how to go about using them; they think they are not very good at sport/exercise, etc.

The biggest risk to health is being INACTIVE.

Reasons behind the advice:
- Protection of vulnerable parts of the body whilst participating (*wear a helmet when cycling or rollerblading; wear protective clothing when playing in goal; wear trainers when skipping or jumping*);
- Protection against the elements (*wear suncream in hot weather; wear layers in cold weather*)
- Avoiding unnecessary injury (*remove jewellery; do not bounce in stretches; warm up before energetic activity; cool down after vigorous exercise; perform curl ups with bent legs*)
- Ensuring that the exercise experience can be sustained and feels comfortable before and after (*drink water before and during energetic exercise; do not exercise immediately after a large meal; work within your limits; shower after sweaty exercise*).

Other ways of maximising the benefits of exercise and minimising the risks might include: avoid extreme arching of the back (*hyperextension*); do not exercise if feeling unwell or ill; always change your clothing before exercise and again afterwards.

TEACHER'S HANDBOOK — Health Related Exercise

Practical

Examples of combining the pulse-raising and mobility parts of the warm-up: performing arm circles or shoulder circles/shrugs/lifts whilst walking or jogging; using arms whilst marching.

It is important that the stretches are related to the activity to follow as this ensures that it is more specific to the muscle groups involved and more likely to be effective in preparing the body and mind for the activity, preventing injury and improving performance.

Depending on the sports or activities on offer and/or selected by the pupils during the lesson, it may be wise to have some rules books handy. Pupils could refer to these to help them answer some of the questions.

Pupils can be encouraged to consider different ways of stretching the same muscle (*eg from: standing; sitting; lying*). An example is the quadriceps stretch which can be performed from standing (*possibly holding onto a wall or partner for support*), from lying on one side, or from lying on one's front. In each case, the main teaching points are the same: knees close together, hip pushed forward, push foot into hand (*not heel into backside*), and avoid arching back.

Brain Teasers

- **Straight-legged sit-ups and standing toe-touches are examples of problem exercises. Why is this? Can you name other problem exercises?**
  Do you know safe alternatives to these exercises?
  Straight-legged sit-ups and standing toe-touches place great stress on the lower part of the back (*lumbar vertebrae*). Other problem exercises include: bouncing in stretches; full and rapid circling of the head; hurdle stretch, etc. Safe alternatives are to: move into and hold stretches still; circle the head slowly and to the front only (*from one shoulder around the front to the other shoulder*); perform a hamstring stretch that does not involve rotating or twisting the knee (*eg sit and reach; lying on back, one leg bent, other leg raised in air, hands behind calf muscle*).

- **How many rules from the same game or from different games can you think of that are designed to minimise risk to players?**
  Rules regarding: kit/dress (*eg no jewellery; wearing of helmets/gloves/pads*); contact (*eg no pushing, no intentional fouls*); duration of play (*half-time, etc*); reprimanding/punishing players (*eg giving out cards; sending players off pitch*), etc.

- **Which sports do you consider to be dangerous?**
  How are accidents and injuries usually avoided in these sports?
  Examples of dangerous sports might be: racing driving; mountain climbing; skiing; etc.
  Accidents and injuries are usually avoided through: initial and continuing training (*eg having lessons; updating knowledge/skills*); wearing of protective clothing/footwear; adherence to strict rules regarding correct procedures, etc.

- **What does '*fairplay*' mean?**
  Fairplay relates to respecting players, the rules and officials, and ensuring a fair, rewarding and enjoyable game (*without cheating or taking unfair advantage*). This helps to maximise the benefits involved in participation (*fun, enjoyment, challenge*) and minimise the risks (*injury, discomfort, pain*).

- **The phrase '*everything in moderation*' can be applied to exercise.**
  What do you think is meant by this?
  Extreme behaviours such as doing no exercise at all or over-training carry risks. Exercise in moderation (*particularly activity that is of at least moderate intensity!*) is health-enhancing, comfortable to perform, rewarding and enjoyable.

GLOSSARY

A

Aerobic activity: Activity which uses the large muscles of the body continuously for extended periods of time (*eg jogging, cycling, swimming, brisk walking, dancing, skipping*). During such activity, oxygen supply is plentiful and energy production takes place in the presence of oxygen.

Anaerobic activity: Activity which is intensive and is carried out over a short period of time (*eg 100 metres sprint, long jump*). During such activity, the energy demands exceed the body's ability to supply sufficient oxygen. Energy production takes place predominantly in the absence of oxygen.

B

Ballistic stretching: Uncontrolled bouncing in stretched positions. Not a recommended method of stretching for most people because of its potential to damage the ends of muscles and to cause soreness and stiffness.

C

Cardiovascular activities/exercises: Activities or exercises which involve large muscle groups and place demands on the ability of the cardiovascular system (*eg heart, blood vessels and circulatory system*) to continue exercising over a period of time.

Cardiovascular health: The condition and efficiency of the cardiovascular system.

Cardiovascular system: The heart, blood vessels and circulatory system. Also referred to as the cardiorespiratory system.

Circuit-training: Circuit-training involves performing a series of exercises in a set sequence.

Cool-down: A process which helps the body to recover from exercise safely and comfortably. An effective cool-down should include pulse lowering exercises and static stretches.

Coronary heart disease: A disease which occurs when the coronary arteries, that supply blood to the heart muscle, become narrowed or blocked.

D

Duration: The length of time spent exercising.

E

Exercise: Physical activity undertaken with a specific objective such as the improvement of fitness, performance or health. Participants may follow a recommended exercise programme detailing frequency (*how often*), intensity (*how hard*), time/duration (*how long*) and mode (*type*) of activity.

F, G

Fitness: Ability to perform physical work satisfactorily. Fitness has many components such as cardiovascular endurance, flexibility, strength, agility, speed, power and reaction time. Fitness is specific, fitness for life differing from fitness for sport.

Flexibility: The range of movement around joints. Flexibility is specific to different joints and is improved through mobility exercises and static stretches.

Frequency: The number of times physical activity is performed.

H

Health: A human condition with physical, social and psychological dimensions. Health can be represented by a continuum ranging from a capacity to enjoy life and to withstand challenges (*positive health*) to morbidity (*disease*) and premature mortality (*negative health*).

Health related exercise (HRE): Exercise that is associated with health benefits such as an improved ability to perform daily activities and a reduced risk of hypokinetic diseases (*those associated with physical inactivity*), such as coronary heart disease. Within an educational context, the term HRE refers to the knowledge, understanding, skills and attitudes considered to be essential for the promotion of an active lifestyle.

Heart rate: The number of times the heart beats in a set period of time (*eg over 15 seconds; over 1 minute*).

High impact activity: Any activity in which both feet leave the floor and the full body weight is absorbed on landing (*eg jogging, running, jumping, leaping*).

I, J, K

Impact: Impact refers to the amount of force on landing.

Intensity: This refers to the demands of the exercise on the participant (*eg how easy or hard the exercise feels*).

L

Lactic acid: A by-product of anaerobic energy production which causes muscle fatigue and soreness.

Loosening exercises: Controlled movements of the joints through their natural range of movement (*eg arm circles, knee lifts*); also known as mobility exercises.

Low impact activity: Any activity in which one foot remains in contact with the floor (*eg walking, marching*).

GLOSSARY

M, N

Maximum heart rate: The maximum rate at which the heart can function. This can be estimated *(over one minute)* by subtracting age from 220.

Mobility or mobilising exercises: Controlled movements of the joints through their natural range of movement *(eg arm circles, knee lifts)*.

Moderate intensity activity: Physical activity which feels fairly demanding but not too tiring, and can be sustained for a period of time; 'activity which makes you begin to huff and puff' *(eg walking, steady jogging)*.

Muscular endurance: The ability of a muscle *(or group of muscles)* to work against a resistance repeatedly *(eg carrying a bench or performing 10 continuous curl-ups)*.

Muscular strength: The maximum amount of force a muscle *(or group of muscles)* can exert against a resistance *(eg lifting a heavy bag or box)*.

Musculo-skeletal health: The condition and efficiency of the bones, joints, muscles, tendons, ligaments and connective tissue.

Musculo-skeletal system: Bones, joints, muscles, tendons, ligaments and connective tissue.

O

Obesity: Excessive amount of body fat.

Osteoporosis: A disease characterised by a reduction in bone mass which increases the risk of fractures.

Overweight: Excess body weight in relation to height.

P, Q, R

Physical activity: This is a broad term that describes any body movement produced by skeletal muscles that results in an increase in energy expenditure *(over the resting rate)*. It includes all forms of movement such as routine activities like housework, gardening and walking, as well as exercise and sport.

Physical fitness: A set of attributes that people have or achieve that relates to the ability to perform physical activity. Some fitness components such as speed, co-ordination and power are related to sports performance. Other fitness components are health related such as cardiorespiratory endurance *(stamina)*, flexibility, muscular strength, muscular endurance, and body composition.

Pulse lowering activities: Rhythmic movements of the large muscle groups that gradually decrease in intensity and help the body to recover from exercise.

Pulse raising activities: Rhythmic movements of the large muscle groups that gradually increase in intensity and prepare the cardiovascular system for more intensive work.

Pulse rate: The number of times the heart beats over a set period of time *(eg over 15 seconds; over one minute)*.

S, T

Sport: Form of physical activity that involves competition and games.

Stamina: The ability to continue performing aerobic exercise for a reasonable period of time. Also known as heart health and cardiorespiratory endurance.

Static stretching: Stretches that are held still. Static stretching is recommended as a safe and effective way of lengthening muscle groups and improving flexibility.

Strength: A general term relating to the ability of muscles to exert and sustain force against a resistance.

Suppleness: A general term relating to the range of movement around joints.

U

Unsafe exercises: Exercises which are likely to incur immediate injury or long-term damage if performed frequently *(eg standing toe touching)*. Sometimes referred to as contra-indicated or controversial exercises.

V

Vigorous intensity activity: Physical activity which feels demanding; 'huff and puff activity' *(eg running fast, jumping)*.

W, X, Y, Z

Warming activities: Activities which gradually raise the pulse and warm the body *(eg walking, marching, jogging)*. Also known as pulse-raising activities.

Warm-up: A process which involves preparing the body gradually and safely for exercise. An effective warm-up should include pulse raising and mobility exercises and short static stretches.

Weight-training: Weight-training involves performing a series of exercises using external weights *(eg barbells)* in a set sequence.

GETTING GOING AND GETTING OVER IT

THE HIGHS AND LOWS OF EXERCISE

HEALTHY HEART HAPPENINGS

Health Related Exercise

OPPORTUNITY KNOCKS

TEACHER'S HANDBOOK

PERFORMING A BALANCING ACT

Author: Dr Jo Harris

Special thanks are due to Dr Lynne Spackman for her invaluable guidance and advice,
ACCAC's Monitoring Group for its interest and support,
staff and pupils of Ysgol Penweddig, Aberystwyth, for their kind co-operation in providing photographic reference material.

© **text:** ACCAC (The Qualifications, Curriculum and Assessment Authority for Wales) 2000

© **illustrations:** ACCAC, **FBA** Publications

All rights reserved. No part of this publication may be reproduced, stored in a retrieval system or transmitted in any form or by means, electronic, mechanical, photocopying, recording or otherwise, without clearance from the copyright holders, ACCAC and **FBA** Publications.

British Library Cataloguing-in-Publication Data.

A catalogue record for this publication is available from the British Library

Published with the financial assistance of ACCAC
(The Qualifications, Curriculum and Assessment Authority for Wales) June 2000

FBA Publications
Number 4, The Science Park
Aberystwyth, Ceredigion SY23 3AH

Tel: 01970 611996 Fax: 01970 625796

Design: **FBA** Aberystwyth

ISBN 1 901862 39 9

9 781901 862393